My Bible

ABC & 123

This book belongs to :

....

....

First Published in 2024
Copyright © 2024 Garren D Williams

ISBN: 978-0-7961-6515-2

Welcome

to the incredible world of "BIBLE ABC & 123"
where you'll join us on an exciting adventure
through the alphabet!
get ready to discover the fascinating stories of
people and events from
the Bible.
Each letter brings us closer to the amazing people
and teachings found in scripture,
Making learning about the Bible fun and
educational.

A a – Adam

Adam and Eve:
Adam and Eve were the very
first people that God created.
They remind us how special each
of us is because God breathed
life into us.

Genesis 2:7

Aa Aa Aa Aa

Aa Aa

B b - Bible

Bible:

The Bible is a very special book that many people around the world believe in.

Its like a guidebook for living a good and happy life.

Bb   Bb   Bb   Bb

Bb   Bb

Creation

Creation:
God created the whole world, and it's filled with such beauty and wonder. From the birds in the sky to the fish in the sea, everything was made by God's loving hands.

Genesis 1:1–31

D d

David

David:
Discover the courageous
shepherd boy who became a
beloved king of Israel, renowned
for his faith, bravery, and his psalms
of worship.

1 Samuel 16–31

Dd Dd Dd Dd Dd Dd

Dd Dd Dd

E e

Easter

Easter:
Easter is a time to celebrate Jesus and all He has done for us. Jesus was sent to earth by God to wash our sins away and not punish us.

John 3:17

Ee Ee Ee Ee

Ee Ee Ee

F f

Fiery furnace

Fiery furnace:
Join Shadrach, Meshach, and Abednego as they face the fiery furnace for refusing to worship a golden idol, and witness God's miraculous protection. Daniel 3

G g

Good – Samaritan

Good Samaritan:
Jesus told a story about a kind person called the Good Samaritan. It teaches us to show love and help others, no matter who they are or where they come from. Luke 10:25-37

H h Heaven

Heaven:
Heaven is a special place that people go to after they leave earth. It's a beautiful and peaceful place where everything is perfect. There are no more tears, pain or sadness, and people get to live in eternal happiness. John 14: 2-4

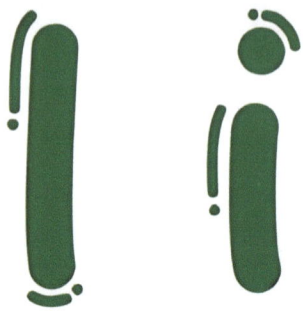

Isaac

I i

GOD Keeps His Promises

Isaac and the Promise:
Isaac was a special child born to
Abraham and Sarah. His birth
showed us that God keeps
His promises, just like He promised
to bless Abraham and Sarah
with a son.

Genesis 21: 1-7

J j

Jesus

Jesus loves children:
Jesus loved spending time with
children and wanted them to
come to Him. He showed us
that children are precious
and loved by God.

Matthew 19:13-15

K k — King Solomon

King Solomon's wisdom:
King Solomon was known for his wisdom and cleverness. He made wise decisions and showed us the importance of seeking wisdom and understanding.

1 kings 1-11

Kk   Kk   Kk   Kk

Kk   Kk

L l

Loaves

Loaves and Fish:
Jesus performed a miracle by feeding five thousand people with only five loaves of bread and two fish. It reminds us that with God, even a little can become more than enough.

Matthew 14:13-21

L L   L L   L L   L L

L L   L L

M m Moses

Moses and the red sea:
Moses led the Israelites out of
slavery in Egypt. God parted the
Rea sea so they could cross safely,
reminding us that God can make
a way when things seem
impossible.

Exodus 14

Mm   Mm   Mm   Mm

Mm   Mm

N n

Noah

Noah's Ark:
God told Noah to build a big ark and fill it with animals to keep them safe during a great flood. It shows us that God always keeps His promises and protects those who believe and trusts in Him.

Genesis 6-9

Nn   Nn   Nn   Nn

Nn   Nn

Olive

Olive branch:
Noah sent out a dove to look for land. An olive branch brought back to Noah by the dove represented peace and the end of the flood. It reminds us that God gives us hope and restores things that were broken.

Genesis 8–11

P p Prayer

Prayer of Hannah:
Hannah prayed to God for a baby, and her prayer was answered. She became a joyful mother and showed us that God listens to our prayers and answers them.

1 Samuel 1-2

Pp   Pp   Pp   Pp

Pp   Pp

Q q

Queen Esther

Queen Esther:
Esther was a brave queen, who saved her people from harm. She showed us that anyone, no matter how small or afraid, can make a big difference with courage.

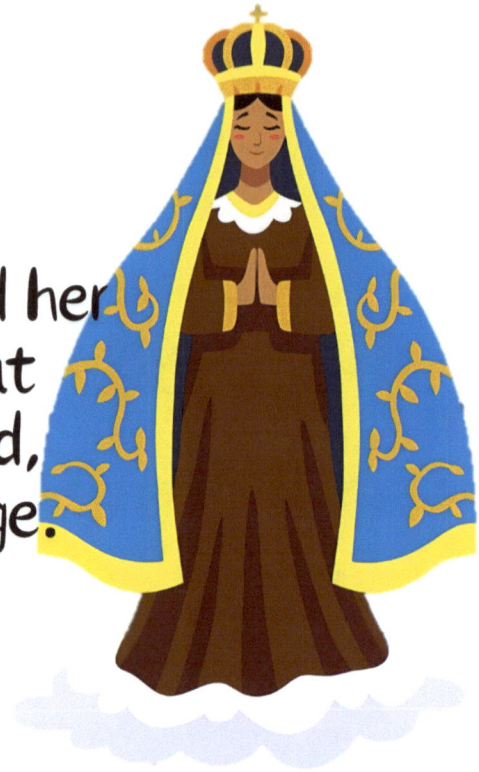

Book of Esther

Qq   Qq   Qq   Qq

Qq   Qq

R r   Resurrection

Resurrection of Jesus:
Jesus rose from the dead after dying on the cross. Its the most incredible event because it means that we can have eternal life with God through Jesus.

Genesis 8–11

Rr   Rr   Rr   Rr

Rr   Rr

S s

Samson

Samson the strong:
Samson was a mighty man with super strength, but he also learnt important lessons about using his strength wisely. His story teaches us about making good choices.

Judges 13–16

Ss   Ss   Ss   Ss

Ss   Ss

T t Ten Commandments

Ten rules for a good life:
God gave Moses ten rules, he called
them ten commandments, to guide
us in living a good and loving life.
They help us so we know how to
treat others and honour God.

Exodus 20: 1-17

U u

Upper room

Upper Room:
The Upper Room was where Jesus shared His last supper with His disciples, teaching about love, humility, and service by washing their feet. Reminding us of His sacrifice and serving others with love and humility. Luke 22: 7-38

U u   U u   U u   U u

u   u

  # Virgin Mary

Virgin Mary:
Mary was chosen by God to be the mother of Jesus, who brought love and salvation to the world. Her story shows us the power of faith and God's plan.

Luke 1: 26-38

   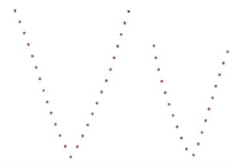

W w <u>W</u>ise Men

Wise men from the East:
The story of the three wise men
following a bright star to find baby
Jesus, presenting Him with gifts
highlights the significance of Jesus'
birth and how God guided them
to Him.

Matthew 2:1-12

Xerxes

Xerxes:
King Xerxes, the mighty Persian ruler recognized for his part in rescuing the Jewish people with Queen Esther's courage. This story highlights how God can work through leaders to protect His people.

Esther 1: 1-3

Y y

Yeshua

Yeshua walks on water:
Also known as Jesus, amazed his disciples by walking on water during a stormy night at sea in Galilee. This teaches us to trust in Jesus even when faced with life's storms, knowing the He is always with us to help and protect us. Matthew 14:22-33

Z z

Zachariah

Zachariah's Angelic Encounter: Zachariah was a priest who was visited by an angel named Gabriel. The Angel told him that he and his wife would have a son named John who will prepare the way for Jesus. This reminds us that nothing is impossible with God

Luke 1:5-25

Z Z Z Z Z

Z Z Z

JESUS

CHRIST

OUR FATHER
WHO ART
IN HEAVEN
HALLOWED
BE THY NAME
THY KINGDOM COME, THY WILL
BE DONE ON EARTH AS IT IS IN HEAVEN
GIVE US THIS DAY OUR DAILY BREAD
AND FORGIVE US OUR TRESSPASSES
AS WE
FORGIVE
THOSE WHO
TRESPASS
AGAINST US
LEAD US
NOT INTO
TEMPTATION
BUT DELIVER
US FROM
EVIL. FOR
THINE IS
THE KINGDOM
THE POWER
AND THE GLORY
FOR EVER
AND EVER
AMEN

One:
There is only <u>One</u> God.

1 1 1 1

ONE GOD

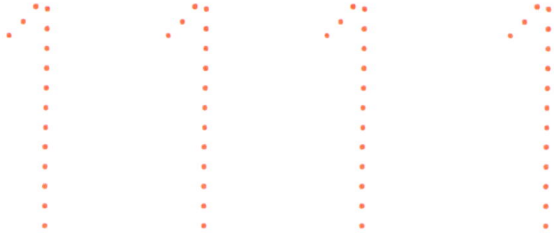

Two:
Noah had two of every animal, male and female on his ark.

2 2 2 2 2

3

Three:
God the Father, God the son and God the holy Spirit.

3 3 3 3

Four:
The Four amazing creatures around God's throne.

In the Book of Revelation, Disciple John saw four amazing creatures – a lion, an ox, a man-like figure, and an eagle

– around God's throne, praising God to depict His greatness and power.

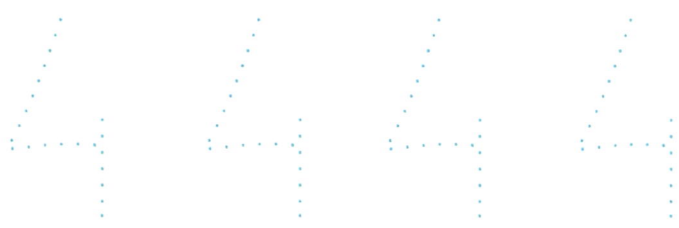

4 4 4 4

4

5

Five:
Jesus shared five loaves of bread and two with five thousand people.

5 5 5 5

Six:
When God created the world, He created us on the sixth day.

6

7

Seven:
When God created the world and us in six days, He rested on the seventh day.

7 7 7 7

Eight:
The eight beatitudes of blessings:

- Blessed are the poor in spirit, for theirs is the kingdom of heaven.
- Blessed are those who mourn, for they will be comforted.
- Blessed are the meek, for they will inherit the earth.
- Blessed are those who hunger and thirst for righteousness, for they will be filled.
- Blessed are the merciful, for they will be shown mercy.
- Blessed are the pure in heart, for they will see God.
- Blessed are the peacemakers, for they will be called children of God.
- Blessed are those who are persecuted because of righteousness, for theirs is the kingdom of heaven.

PEACEMAKERS

MERCIFUL

PURE OF HEART

8

8 8 8 8

9

Nine:
The nine fruits of the spirit

Charity, Joy, Goodness, Patience, Kindness, Faithfulness, Generosity, Peace and Modesty

Ten:
The ten commandments:

- "You shall have no other gods before me"
- "You shall not make yourself an idol or worship any other gods."
- "You shall not take the name of the Lord your God in vain." .
- "Remember the sabbath day and keep it holy."
- "Honor your father and mother."
- "You shall not kill."
- "You shall not commit adultery."
- "You shall not steal." ...

- "You shall not lie"
- " You shall not covet"

Thank you!

Thank you for taking this journey with us.
We hope you had fun and learnt wonderful new things about the Bible.
We must always pray to GOD and say thank you for all GOD does for us, our family and friends.

Prayer:

Thank you God for the world so sweet,
Thank you God for the food we eat,
Thank you God for the Birds that sing,
Thank you, God, for everything.

God, we thank you for the night,
and for the pleasant morning light;
For rest and food and loving care,
and all that makes the day so fair.
Help us to do the things we should,
to be to others kind and good;
In all we do, in work or play,
to grow more loving every day.
AMEN!

Acknowledgements:

Images / illustrations attributions:

ministry-to-children.com

pixabay.com

freepik.com